BALL

W9-BIU-532

BALL

BALL

Ripley's Believe It or Not!

Developed and produced by Ripley Publishing Ltd

This edition published and distributed by:
Mason Crest Publishers Inc.
370 Reed Road, Broomall, Pennsylvania 19008
(866) MCP-BOOK (toll free)
www.masoncrest.com

Copyright © 2004 by Ripley Entertainment Inc. This edition printed in 2010.
All rights reserved. Ripley's, Believe It or Not!, and Ripley's Believe It or Not!
are registered trademarks of Ripley Entertainment Inc.

Ripley's Believe It or Not!
All Consuming
ISBN 978-1-4222-1536-4
Library of Congress Cataloging-in-Publication data is available

Ripley's Believe It or Not!—Complete 16 Title Series
ISBN 978-1-4222-1529-6

No part of this publication may be reproduced in whole or in part, or stored in a retrieval
system, or transmitted in any form or by any means, electronic, mechanical,
photocopying, recording, or otherwise, without written permission from the publishers.
For information regarding permission, write to VP Intellectual Property, Ripley
Entertainment Inc., Suite 188, 7576 Kingspointe Parkway, Orlando, Florida, 32819
email: publishing@ripleys.com

PUBLISHER'S NOTE
While every effort has been made to verify the accuracy of the entries in this book,
the Publishers cannot be held responsible for any errors contained in the work.
They would be glad to receive any information from readers.

WARNING
Some of the stunts and activities in this book are undertaken by experts and should not
be attempted by anyone without adequate training and supervision.

Printed in the United States of America

Ripley's Believe It or Not!

ALL-CONSUMING

Ripley PUBLISHING

a Jim Pattison Company

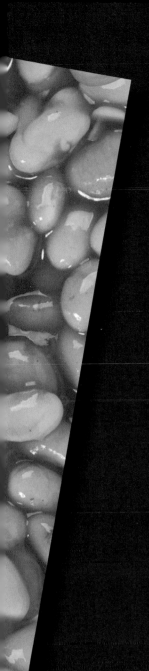

All-Consuming

Open wide... Are you bonkers about beans,

addicted to sugar, or just like playing with your

food? Feast your eyes on the fashionable food

that you can actually wear, try and stop your

tongue tingling when you read about the Stinging

Nettle Eating Championships, and find out what

can be done with your chewing gum after it's

lost its flavor.

Meet Captain Beany, who lives his life
as a baked bean...

Man of bEaNs

Captain Beany lives his life as a baked bean. The tomato sauce-soaked food gets his pulse racing so much that he regularly plunges into a bathtub full of them.

BARRY KIRK, AKA CAPTAIN BEANY, is bean mad! In fact he loves baked beans so much that he has officially changed his name to Captain Beany.

He drives a baked–bean illustrated car, drinks baked–bean cocktails, paints himself orange, and dons a baked–bean costume! He wears an orange jumpsuit and cape and even paints his bald head orange. When he needed a passport to match his new identity, he produced a completely orange photo of himself. Naturally, he eats baked beans every day.

Bean Feats

In June 2004, Hollywood celebrated the 30th anniversary of the blockbuster movie *Blazing Saddles*, by producing a special edition DVD promotion. The event was happily celebrated at the Saddle Ranch Chop House in the heart of Hollywood and was marked with a human "bean dip" contest. Movie fans took turns to dive in and search through the beans for a *Blazing Saddles* DVD.

A stalwart Blazing Saddles *fan scrambles in a vat of baked beans for the DVD.*

Claiming to hail from Planet Beanus, on Earth Captain Beany uses a mode of transport that is much more suitable for human "beans."

His motto is "to baldly go where no man has bean before" and to that end he founded the New Millennium Bean Party, polling 122 votes in the 2001 general election.

The 50-year-old Captain, who recently paid $750 to insure himself against alien abduction, plans to turn his apartment in Port Talbot, South Wales, into a bean museum. However, there is a downside to being Captain Beany. "I've been out of work since 1992," says Kirk, "because I've changed my name and dress up as Captain Beany. . . a job for a superhero is very hard to come by." Just don't let anyone call him a "has-bean!"

Bean Bathtub
Danny Cooper, a computer student from Kings Lynn, England, raised money for charity by immersing himself for two hours in a bathtub full of cold baked beans.

MGH 726L

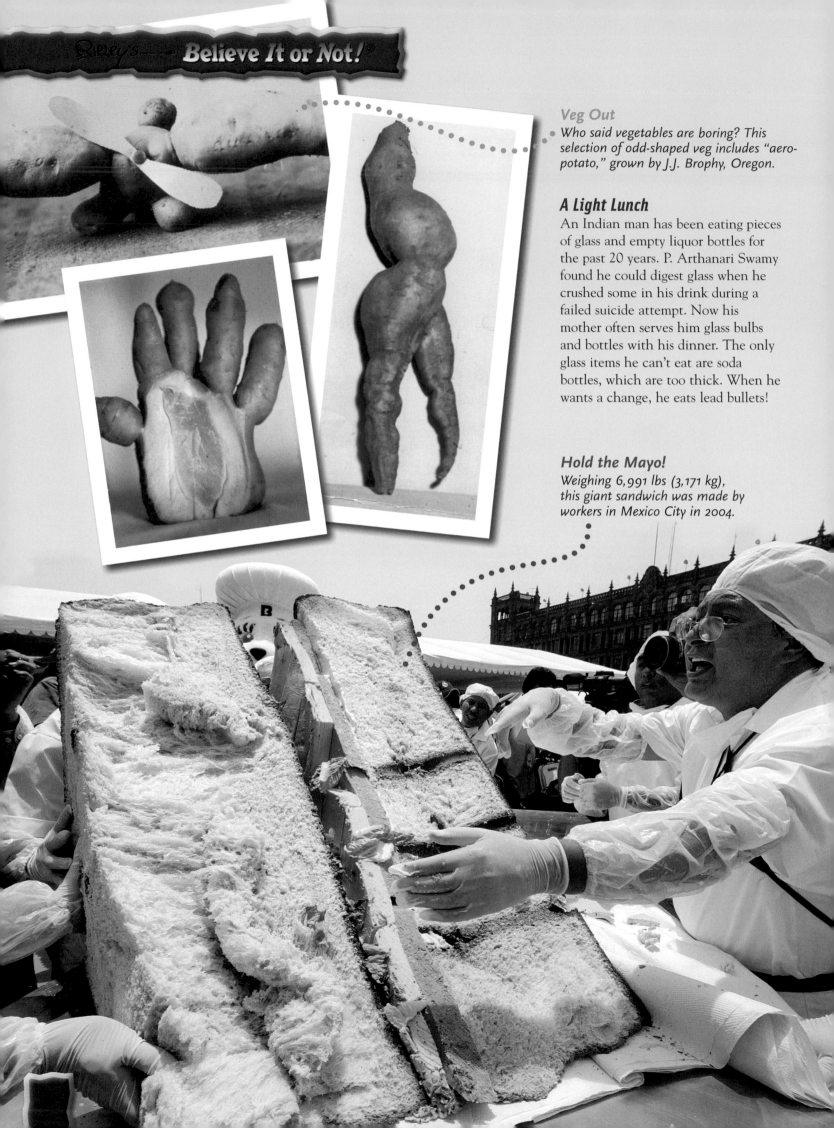

Veg Out

Who said vegetables are boring? This selection of odd-shaped veg includes "aero-potato," grown by J.J. Brophy, Oregon.

A Light Lunch

An Indian man has been eating pieces of glass and empty liquor bottles for the past 20 years. P. Arthanari Swamy found he could digest glass when he crushed some in his drink during a failed suicide attempt. Now his mother often serves him glass bulbs and bottles with his dinner. The only glass items he can't eat are soda bottles, which are too thick. When he wants a change, he eats lead bullets!

Hold the Mayo!

Weighing 6,991 lbs (3,171 kg), this giant sandwich was made by workers in Mexico City in 2004.

Bearing Fruit
Camilla Bowitz from Worcester, England, had a special fruit tree growing in her back garden—it bore both apples and plums!

Don't Forget to Floss
Diane DeCair of Toledo, Ohio, likes to inhale strands of spaghetti up her nose. In fact, by carefully sniffing and coughing, she can simultaneously pull one end of the pasta from her nose and the other from her mouth, in a flossing motion. "It's kind of disgusting to watch," she admits.

The Spitting Image
The International Cherry Pit Spitting Championship at Eau Claire, Michigan, has turned into a real family affair. Rick Krause has won the title 12 times, and in 2004 his son Brian completed a hat-trick of wins with a spit of 88 ft 2 in (26.8 m), just 5 ft (1.5 m) short of his 2003 record. Rick actually married his wife Marlene at the contest. Naturally, she's an ace spitter too.

Forever Blowing Bubbles
Susan Montgomery Williams of Fresno, California, has been America's "Bubble Queen" since 1979. After discovering that the existing record for blowing bubblegum was a modest 17 in (43 cm) bubble, Susan told the Bubble Yum Company that she could blow a 20 in (50 cm) bubble with just three pieces of gum. They didn't believe her, until she arrived blowing a bubble the size of a basketball with one breath. She won an unlimited supply of bubblegum as long as she held the record. Over 25 years later, she still holds it with a blow of 23 in (58 cm).

U.S.A.
Maine
In Portland, shoelaces must be tied while walking down the street.

Make Yourself at Home
A burglar broke into a dozen Seattle homes in August 2004 to raid… the fridges. Ignoring the jewelry, in one home he ate six shrimp kebabs, 12 mini corndogs, half a pack of cooked meat, 12 balls of frozen cookie dough, handfuls of candies, a box of Creamsicles, two fruit drinks, and a glass of milk. In another break-in he thawed and fried frozen steaks and ate them while watching TV—until he was disturbed by the homeowners!

Dip In

While 20 per cent of the U.S.A.'s population eat 48 per cent of the avocados consumed each year, Super Bowl Sunday is the biggest day of the year for avocado consumption. Industry executives estimate that more than 43 million lb (19.5 million kg) are eaten during the football game, most of it in the form of guacamole dip.

Dog Eat Dog

At age ten, "Krazy" Kevin Lipsitz from Staten Island, New York, could eat ten ears of corn in a sitting. Now a speed-eating champ, he once ate 2 lbs (1 kg) of sour pickles in five minutes, and his wife, Lorain, also competes as "Loraineasaurus Rex." Kevin trains with his two dogs. "I cook up a family pack of 40 hot dogs and we race. But we don't eat out of the same bowl."

Impeccable Taste

Wilma Beth Shulke of Mission, Texas, created her own Easter outfit made from sliced cross-sections of corn cobs, trimmed with orange peel.

A Brush with Death

Surgeons in India removed a toothbrush from a man's stomach a week after he accidentally swallowed it. Anil Kumar apparently swallowed the toothbrush while brushing his teeth in front of the TV, but only went to the hospital when the pain became unbearable.

Hair-brained Scheme

Gary Arnold has a unique method of charging customers who visit his restaurant in Lodi, California—he charges them according to the amount of hair on their head. The hairiest pay most, and bald people eat for free!

Sweet as Candy

Slater Barron's friends and neighbors collect lint for her, which she stores in boxes in her studio/garage. She then sorts the lint according to color before creating the art.

Ripley's®
LINT ART
EXHIBIT NO: 13989
SUSHI AND CANDY MADE BY SLATER BARRON
ENTIRELY OUT OF LINT

DRESSING for DINNER

FASHION DESIGNER Alessandro Consiglio cooked up a storm on the runways of Rome, Italy, in 2002.

Using vacuum-packed meat (including salami, ham, and pastrami) instead of conventional fabrics, the exotic fashion designer created a feast for more than just the eyes as models showed off the meaty masterpieces to applauding onlookers.

Consiglio's dresses are made from many different types of salami and ham.

Bread Winner

As part of his Pain Couture *exhibition in Paris, fashion designer Jean Paul Gaultier celebrated the artistry of French bakers by creating dresses, boots, bags, and even thongs, from dough.*

Speak for Yourself

Known as "Bread Head," Japanese artist Tatsumi Orimoto spent June 1996 strolling through London with baguettes tied to his head. Earlier, he had spent two years in Germany with a 9-ft (3-m) chimney in his backpack and five years with a cardboard box on his foot. He passed another year dragging an iron bath round New York's Greenwich Village. "It's my way of communicating," he says.

11

Gross Interest

Whereas most people like to pop chocolate into their mouth, John LaMedica prefers live cockroaches. The man known as "Jungle John" stuffed a record nine poisonous Madagascan cockroaches into his mouth at the same time during a *Ripley's Believe It Or Not!* TV show in 2003. John, from Newark, Delaware, admits his act is "really gross." He adds: "They hiss and have spikes on their legs that cut the inside of my mouth, and sometimes they defecate in your mouth, but you can't do much about it. It leaves a bitter taste."

Chew it Over

Seattle's unlikeliest tourist attraction is the Gum Wall in Pike Place Market. The entire wall is covered in thousands of pieces of chewing-gum in all colors from the mouths of people from all over the world.

Breaking Bread

A church in Buffalo, New York, has decided that visitors should be able to grab lunch while worshiping. The True Bethel Baptist Church is the first in the U.S.A. to open its own Subway restaurant.

Radiator Grill

Dave Curtis of Suffolk, England, converted his Skoda car into a wheely unusual barbecue!

Chickening Out

Kay Martin freaked out when the chicken she was cooking began to squawk. Steam had built up in the bird and was escaping through its vocal cords. Put off, Martin threw it out and hasn't cooked chicken since.

Champion Biscuit

The world's biggest ham biscuit was prepared at Smithfield, Virginia, in 2002. Made from 500 lbs (230 kg) of ham, it measured a staggering 8 ft wide and 14 in (36 cm) tall.

Don't Bug Me

Students at the Iowa State University Entomology Club don't just study six-legged bugs, they also eat them! Particular favorite accompaniments are a cajun sauce, covered in chocolate—or just dipped in Jell-O.

Ice-breakers

In a bid to boost sales, Japanese confectioners introduced an exciting new range of ice-creams in 2002. Customers could cool down with such exotic flavors as octopus, horseradish, shark's fin, garlic, potato and lettuce, whale, and cactus, not to mention basashi vanilla, which contained chunks of raw horse-flesh! Meanwhile, a British restaurateur has started serving bacon-and-egg ice-cream.

Some of the exotic ice-cream flavors the Japanese invented during the scorching summer of 2002.

BY GUM!

- Between 1992 and 2004, chewing-gum was banned in Singapore as it messed up streets and trains. Gum dealers face jail if they break the rules

- In 2003, students at a school in Washington persuaded teachers to let them chew gum in class because scientific tests showed that it increased the blood flow to brain cells

- Furious at seeing the Russian soccer team chewing gum rather than singing the national anthem at Euro 2004, President Putin ordered all gum in Russia to be confiscated

Dead as a Dodo

Benjie Moss, a student at Staffordshire University in England, created this life-sized sculpture of the long-extinct Dodo bird after he gave up smoking and started chewing gum to alleviate his cravings. Rather than discarding the gum, he put it to good use making this sculpture!

Long-distance Call

When you visit a McDonald's drive-thru, no matter where you are, it's quite possible that your order is routed through a call center in Colorado Springs, Colorado. Within 30 seconds, the order you shout into the microphone is typed into a computer in Colorado and then routed back to that same McDonald's kitchen. The system apparently creates fewer errors.

Emergency Rations

A U.S. Army laboratory has developed a dried meal that can be hydrated with dirty water or, if absolutely necessary, a soldier's own urine. This is possible because a special membrane allows only water molecules to pass through and filters out more than 99 per cent of bacteria and most chemicals.

Gum Blondes

Artist Jason Kronenwald, from Toronto, Ontario, creates portraits of celebrities that appear to be made out of clay but are actually sculpted from chewing-gum. He doesn't like to chew gum himself, but instead persuades his friends to soften it up for his use. His *Gum Blondes* series includes singer Britney Spears and actress Pamela Anderson.

Great Britney

Britney Spears' fans clearly don't think the pop star's chewed gum is toxic—because they bought some of it on eBay. On the Internet site in September 2004, there were more than two dozen auctions of chewing-gum, which people claimed had been spat out by Britney. Most pieces sold for around $50, although fake bidding almost pushed the price as high as $14,000!

Having a Ball

Eric "Badlands" Booker, a 34-year-old 395-lb (180-kg) heavyweight has for the second year in a row, become the Matzo Ball Contest champ. In 2003, Booker earned a world record by wolfing down 21 of the baseball-size dumplings, which are made from meal, eggs, and chicken broth. In 2004, the subway operator gobbled up just 20 of the 5-oz (140-g) balls in the allotted 5 minutes 25 seconds, but still won. He prepared by eating 10 lbs (4.5 kg) of cabbage three nights before the contest.

Nutty Protester

To demonstrate his support for English culture and food, performance artist Mark McGowan decided to turn himself into a full English breakfast. For 12 days in November 2003, McGowan sat in a London shop window in a bath of baked beans, with two chips up his nose and 48 sausages wrapped around his head. Earlier in the year, he had protested against student debt by using his nose to roll a peanut along 7 mi (11 km) of London roads to the Prime Minister's door at 10 Downing Street.

A Colossal Appetite

In 1999, pizza-maker Jeff Parker from Brooks in Alberta, Canada, came up with the world's biggest commercially available pizza. Called the "Colossal," it measures 3 ft (90 cm) wide and 4 ft (1.2 m) long, and serves 108 people.

My Head's Spinning

Now you can wash your dirty laundry in public and drink a cocktail at the same time! The Laundry Bar in Miami, Florida, is an ordinary laundromat but it also has a fully stocked and licensed bar.

U.S.A.
Georgia

No one may carry an ice-cream cone in their back pocket on a Sunday.

The Tipping Point

A 2003 survey of Domino's Pizza managers in the Washington D.C. area found that the day Saddam Hussein was captured, December 13, 2003, was the biggest day of the year for tips, and orders for meat-topped pies were the highest in two years.

To Diet For

No willpower? Then "DDS," a new dental appliance, might help. The dental plate fits on the roof of the mouth and prevents people from shoveling in large quantities of food. One study has shown the $400 device helped people to lose more than 1 lb (0.5 kg) a week.

Wakey Wakey

A Minnesota dairy has begun producing milk that is spiked with caffeine. Called "Hyper Cow," the frothy breakfast staple contains as much caffeine and sugar as a can of soda.

Bean Feast

Tracy Ostmann loves to make jellybean art. She was once commissioned to create a jellybean painting of a great white shark for a Chicago aquarium. More recently, she produced a 15-color portrait of Martin Luther King Jr. While Ostmann loves her medium, she says she has to refrain from eating too many of the beans while working, just in case she makes herself sick.

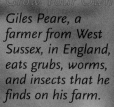

Grow Your Own

Giles Peare, a farmer from West Sussex, in England, eats grubs, worms, and insects that he finds on his farm.

No Licking!

THE WORLD'S FIRST—and only—hotel made entirely of salt has a "no licking" policy.

Built on the world's largest salt bed, the Uyuni Salt Hotel is located west of Colchani, deep in the salt plains of Bolivia, South America. Passing the salt will never be a problem, as the salt will always be on the table—in fact, like everything else, the table is made of salt.

Vinegar Joes

Vinegar-lovers gather in South Dakota, for the annual Vinegar Festival. Top prize goes to the Mother of All Vinegars contest winner. There's also a tasting at the vinegar museum—sugar cubes are then supplied to freshen contestants' mouths.

The Uyuni Salt Hotel is the only hotel in the world that is made entirely from salt.

Even the hotel beds are made from salt crystals.

On Ice

An 81-year-old Indian woman has eaten huge chunks of ice every day for the last 17 years to relieve stomach ache. Shanti Devi eats up to 22 lbs (10 kg) a day in the summer, and says she can't sleep without her daily ice intake, most of it from neighbors' refrigerators.

Pizza the Action

In August 1998, a company called Little Caesar's took an order from jeans manufacturer the VF Corporation of Greensboro, North Carolina, for 13,386 pizzas—to feed 40,160 employees at 180 locations in the U.S.A.

Fungi Fun

Weighing over 21 lbs (9.5 kg), this edible giant puffball fungus was discovered by A.B. Tyler near his home in New York.

BEAN SCENE

- The navy bean got its name because it was an essential part of the US Navy's diet in the 19th century

- The navy bean is the official vegetable of Massachusetts

- A restaurant dedicated solely to the culinary delights of baked navy beans opened in Melbourne, Australia, in 2004

- Native Americans flavored their baked navy beans with maple syrup

- West Bromwich, England, has been dubbed The Windy City after a survey found its inhabitants to be the UK's biggest fans of baked beans

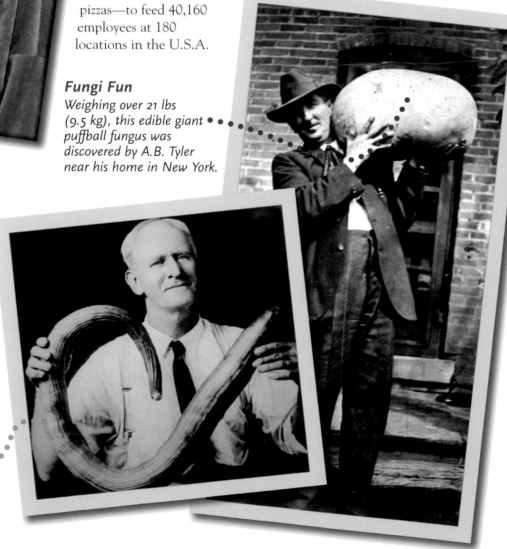

Sugar Sugar

Mary Horton is addicted to sugar—she eats an average of 2 lbs (1 kg) of it every day!

A Big Fish

By swallowing 350 live minnows in under an hour, Shane Williams of Wonder Lake, Chicago, smashed the existing record of 280 set in 1998.

Naked Lunch?

At Germany's Bellview Restaurant the menus are painted on the bare skin of the waiters and waitresses.

Super Cucumber

Willian H. Rainey of Fort Worth, Texas grew a cucumber to an amazing 4 ft 11 in (1.4 m)!

Bean Cuisine

After taking part in a bean cook-off, contestants in the annual Bean Fest at Mountain View, Arkansas, then compete in an "outhouse race."

Stab in the Pack

A Michigan housewife was rushed to the hospital after accidentally stabbing herself with a shard of pasta. It entered her finger with such force that doctors had to remove part of her fingernail.

Shell Shock

Norwegian Rune Naeri swallowed 187 oysters in three minutes—more than one per second—at the 2003 Hillsborough Oyster Festival in Northern Ireland. His total almost doubled the previous world record.

Biting the Bullet

Eating a hot dog in May 2004, Californian Olivia Chanes bit on something hard. When she began complaining of a metallic taste in her mouth, doctors discovered that she had swallowed a 0.4 in (9 mm) bullet!

The Worms Turn

In November 2003, C. Manoharan swallowed 200 live earthworms in just 20 seconds on a beach in the Indian port of Chennai. Each worm was 4 in (10 cm) long, and it took him a year to prepare for the feat.

Sourpusses!

A St. Louis health commissioner has apologized to Mim Murray, 10, and Marisa Miller-Stockie, 12, after a city inspector shut down their lemonade stand for operating without a business license. The girls were just trying to raise money to buy laptop computers. The city later admitted that it was overzealous in its attempt to enforce its food and vendor permit rules.

Ice and a Slice?
This giant lemon grew in a hot house in Chippenham, England. Compared to this ordinary-sized lemon, it sure is a whopper!

COFFEE BREAK

- In 17th-century Turkey, anyone who was caught drinking coffee was executed

- According to Harvard research, regular coffee-drinkers have less chance of having asthma

- The Japanese bathe in ground coffee to improve their skin

Spam Cram

First held in 1978, Spamara attracts thousands of Spamophiles to Austin, Texas, to an annual celebration of the famous tinned meat. Events include a Spam toss, a Spam-calling contest, and a Spam-eating competition, known as the "Spam Cram."

Eggstra Large

Take more than 5,000 eggs, add 50 lb (23 kg) of onions, 75 green bell peppers, 52 lb (24 kg) of butter, over 6 gal (23 l) of milk, 4 gal (15 l) of green onion tops, 2 gal (8 l) of parsley, some crawfish tails, and Tabasco pepper sauce to taste, and what have you got?... the Giant Omelette of Abbeville, Louisiana, which keeps on getting bigger each year. The Giant Omelette Celebration began in 1984 with 5,000 eggs, and one egg has been added every year since.

Toe Sandwich

A 35-year-old Austrian man, hungry for a snack, hacked off the toes on his left foot, fried them, and ate them between two slices of bread—because he could find nothing else to eat! When ambulance staff arrived, the man offered a toe, saying it tasted like chicken!

U.S.A. Georgia

In Gainesville, chicken may only legally be eaten using ones fingers instead of cutlery.

Burns' Night Blast-off

In 2002, Canadian businessman Gordon Sinclair announced that, as part of the Robert Burns' Night celebrations, he had patented a Haggis Launcher in order to propel a 1 lb (454 g) haggis across Calgary's huge Bow River!

A Sting in the Tale

Dorset, England, is home to the World Stinging Nettle Eating Championships, in which competitors eat their way through the stinging, itching plant. Ouch!

Eat Your Art Out
Forget paints—this carpet is being painted with food including cream and custard!

Eating Around the World
While he was rating the quality of diners around the world, Chicago food critic Fred E. Magel visited 46,000 restaurants in 60 countries over a period of 50 years.

There's the Grub
A Thai firefighter named Paisit Chanta thinks the key to a healthy life is to eat a live worm every single day. He has done so for 30 years and says that he has suffered nothing worse than mild flu.

Let Them Eat Cake
Drew Cerza, of Buffalo, New York, came up with a way to help others unload their unwanted holiday fruitcakes without tossing them in the trash. He asked for 100,000 cakes to be sent to him so that he could forward them to a food bank for the needy. His only stipulation was that the fruitcake be no more than two years old.

Double Trouble
An Israeli woman swallowed a fork in 2003 while trying to retrieve a cockroach from her throat. The insect jumped into her mouth while she was brushing her teeth, but when she tried to scoop it out with a fork, she swallowed that too.

It's No Turkey
Seattle soft drinks firm Jones Soda Co. introduced a turkey-and-gravy flavored fizzy drink for Christmas 2003. The novelty line proved to be so successful that it very quickly sold out, leaving thirsty customers clamoring for more.

When the Chips are Down
Nicknamed a "compulsive swallower," a man in the 1930s was reported to have swallowed several poker chips. This X-ray shows the chips inside the man's stomach.

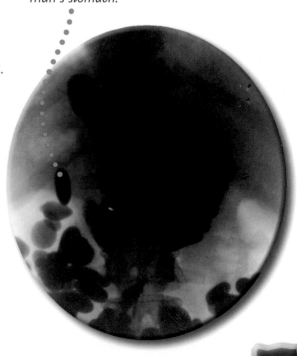

Mouse Trap
In the 1940s, Dagmar Rothman performed a stunt at Ripley's New York City Odditorium in which he swallowed lemons and a mouse—and then regurgitated them.

UMmm... NiCE!?!

Matthew gets stuck on to a chewy treat.

MATTHEW BIANCANIELLO proved that he can eat anything during a 2002 *Ripley's* TV show.

Matthew's feat is not for the weak-stomached to watch! His eat-anything menu includes such treats as animal eyeballs, cow dung, a cow's and bull's muscles, leeches, maggots, and fish intestines.

Matthew considers the many delicacies he intends to devour during his act.

Grubs, maggots, and worms... delicious!

I believe that's an eyeball he's eating!

Matthew takes a pause before consuming yet another sumptuous snack!

Delivering the Goods

In 1998, Manhattan restaurant-owner Eddie Fishbaum was asked to deliver a plain pizza to TV host Eiji Bando in Tokyo, a distance of 6,753 mi (10,868 km). The pizza cost $7,000 including Eddie's airfare.

Brain Box

Etta's Lunch Box Café in Logan, Ohio, is decorated with owner Ladora Ouesley's collection of more than 400 lunchboxes. If customers point out the type of box they used to carry to school, Ladora can correctly identify the year they began their education.

Bite Size

Philadelphia confectioner Glenn Mueller Jr. has introduced a line of chocolate body parts. Enjoy the smooth texture of chocolate hearts, brains, lungs, and even dentures. If you can't resist one naughty bite, try the Mike Tyson special—a chocolate ear with a chunk missing!

Human Piggy Bank

When treated for stomach pains, a 62-year-old Frenchman was found to have swallowed 350 coins (francs and euros), plus assorted necklaces and needles. They weighed 12 lbs (5 kg), as much as a bowling ball. The man, who died shortly afterwards, had been swallowing coins for ten years despite his family's attempts to wean him off them.

Fowl Play

A two-hour jail riot which resulted in an estimated $10,000-worth of damage was sparked by the poor quality of a chicken dinner! Inmates at Autry State Prison in Pelham, Georgia, smashed lights, destroyed sprinkler heads, broke windows, and set fire to mattresses in December 2001 after one of the prisoners complained that his chicken was not thoroughly cooked.

Knit Wit

Eileen Mulrooney made a special kind of cake for her daughter's wedding. It looked yummy, but eating it wouldn't have been a pleasant experience—the whole cake was made from knitted wool!

Lord of the Flies

A man named Farook has taken to eating a diet consisting solely of flies in protest at his council's garbage-collection service. The social worker says that garbage left in the streets of Tirunelveli, western India, is attracting swarms of the insects.

Piece of Cake

Training instructor Robert Jones cut his 50th birthday cake while doing a one-handed handstand. Other feats included doing a handstand with 200 lb (90 kg) of weights tied around his waist.

Hen-pecked

Jan Csovary from Prievidza, Slovakia, has eaten more than 11,000 chickens since being diagnosed as a diabetic in the early 1970s. He has chicken for breakfast, lunch, and tea, but has to cook it himself because his wife moaned that she was sick of the sight of chickens 20 years ago!

Spuds they Like

Every year, the town of Clark, South Dakota, stages a Potato Day in celebration of its favorite vegetable. The festivities include a Best Decorated Potato contest, potato sculptures and mashed-potato wrestling, in which the combatants fight each other in a ring full of mashed potato.

EXTRA PEPPERONI?

- There are approximately 61,300 pizzerias in the U.S.A. and over 9,000 in New York alone

- 94 per cent of the population of the U.S.A. eat pizza

- Americans eat about 100 acres (40 ha) of pizza each day, or about 350 slices per second

- Americans eat 251,770,000 lbs (114,201,000 kg) of pepperoni, their favorite pizza topping, every year

- Red herring is the most popular pizza topping in Russia

- Unusual toppings created by pizza-makers include peanut butter and jelly, bacon and eggs, and mashed potatoes

Big Mouth

In 1998, American Johnny Reitz managed to cram three standard-sized hamburgers (including buns) into his mouth simultaneously without swallowing.

Beat That

Omelette fans had better head to Norma's, a restaurant in a hotel in Manhattan, New York, which sells a $1,000 "Zillion Dollar Frittata," surely the most expensive in the world. Made with six eggs, a whole lobster, and 10 oz (283 g) of caviar, the omelette started out as a simple Lobster Frittata. Chef Emile Castillo and the hotel's general manager Steven Pipes decided to experiment with different ingredients and soon discovered that adding caviar made it even more delicious. Its entry on the menu dares customers to experience it.

A "budget" version of the omelette is also available, which contains only 1 oz (28 g) of caviar and sells for $100.

The Breakfast Club

Since 1990, Springfield, Massachusetts, has been home to the world's largest pancake breakfast, at which an 1,800-ft (549-m) long table seats more than 75,000 people. The feast requires 2,700 lbs (1,225 kg) of flour, 600 lbs (272 kg) of eggs, 210 lbs (95 kg) of butter, and 210 gal (795 l) of water, all topped with 450 gal (1,703 l) of maple syrup. The pancakes are served with 3,370 gal (12,757 l) of coffee and 1,150 gal (4,353 l) of orange juice.

On the Double

On October 11, 2004, Domino's Pizza offered a free medium double crust pizza to any New Yorker who could prove that they had the same first and last name. Via an online search, Domino's estimated that there were at least 30 locals who would be able to take advantage of the offer.

Winging it

Ed "Cookie" Jarvis is a man of taste. In fact, the speed-eater from Long Island, New York, holds records for consuming such diverse items as ice-cream, pasta, pork ribs, corned beef, and cabbage. He has also eaten 91 Chinese dumplings in eight minutes, 40 meatballs in four minutes, and 2 lbs (907 g) of pickles in five minutes. He beat champion eater Sonya Thomas in a chicken-wing contest when he devoured 134 in just 12 minutes!

Choices, Choices

La Casa Gelato, in Vancouver, certainly knows ice-cream. The store offers customers nearly 500 flavors, although only 208 are available at any given time. Diversity in flavors apparently keeps customers coming back for more. The range includes such exotic tastes as curry, corn, durian, blue cheese, dandelion, garlic, vinegar, wasabi/green apple—and one that tastes like Guinness stout.

Big Cheese

Sculptors Jimm Scannell and Jim Victor created a life-sized replica of a race car using 3,500 lbs (1,600 kg) of Cheddar cheese for the International Speedway in Richmond, Virginia.

Keen as Mustard

The first Saturday in August is Official Mustard Day in Mount Horeb, Wisconsin. Now in its 15th year, the celebration, held at the local mustard museum, features mustard tastings and a fiery cook-off.

HARD CHEESE

- Cheese was a form of currency in 16th-century Denmark

- A 1956 expedition to the South Pole found a tin of Edam cheese left behind by Captain Scott and his party in 1912. The cheese was still edible

- Blue Vinny cheese is so hard that a whole cheese was once used as a temporary wheel replacement on a train

- Cornish Yarg cheese is served coated in nettles

- In the 12th century, Blanche of Navarre tried to win the heart of the French king Philippe Auguste by sending him 200 cheeses every year

Carrot and Stick

Julie Tori from Southampton, England, has eaten between 4 lbs (1.8 kg) and 5 lbs (2.3 kg) of carrots every day for the past ten years. She did have one day off from munching her favorite vegetable but was immediately seized by a panic attack.

Dynamic Duo

According to a recent survey by Mr. Clean and Magic Eraser, Americans simply can't resist spaghetti and meatballs. The dish took the title for "Favorite Food Duo," and macaroni and cheese, and milk and cereal were a close second and third.

Choc Tactics

This sculpture should have chocoholics watering at the mouth. Tokyo chef Daisuke Nogami took one month and used 550 lbs (250 kg) of white chocolate to create an 80-in (203-cm) tall replica of the Venus de Milo statue. It was displayed at the Food Art Museum in Tokyo in 2003.

Pie in the Sky

According to Domino's Pizza, the five biggest days for pizza delivery in the U.S.A. are Super Bowl Sunday, Thanksgiving Eve, New Year's Day, New Year's Eve, and Halloween. Every week, Domino's drivers rack up 9 million mi (13.5 million km), which is further than 37 trips to the Moon and back.

Hard Graft

Paramedics in Stuart, Florida, worked up a sweat when trying to remove a 480-lb (218-kg) woman from her home. They knew the doorways would be tricky, but quickly discovered a much more pressing problem. The woman, who had not moved from her couch for several years, had to be carried out on it because the fabric had grafted on to her skin. Doctors surgically separated the woman from the couch, but she died in the hospital after breathing complications.

Yellow Peril

Californian Ken Bannister, known as "Banana Man," has amassed more than 17,000 banana-related objects since he founded the International Banana Club in 1972. He has a banana-shaped putter and yellow golf balls; books on bananas; a banana-shaped couch; banana-related art, clothing, food, and toiletries; plus banana-shaped telephones, lamps, clocks, watches, soft toys, crockery, and cutlery!

In the Soup

In Erie, Pennsylvania, Democrats at the Polish Falcons Club eat duck blood soup every election day!

Say Cheese!

Offbeat Canadian sculptor Cosimo Cavallaro doesn't work with ordinary art materials—he uses cheese! He has dressed a model from head to toe in cheese, sprayed jackets in cheese, and decorated a New York hotel room with dripping formaggio. In 2001, he even painted an entire house in Wyoming with 10,000 lbs (4,500 kg) of sprayed-on mozzarella. Then, in 2004, to prove that he could work with other materials, he covered a bed at a Manhattan hotel with slices of a 308-lb (140-kg) processed ham.

It's Electrifying

It was an illuminating experience for Russian Alvarez Kanichka when he swallowed live lightbulbs—and then retrieved them by pulling on the electrical cord, still attached!

Seedy Art

New York artist Hugh McMahon loves to create art with watermelons. Weighing up to 50 lbs (23 kg), most pieces take him two hours to complete.

Eat My Shorts

Stopped by cops, an 18-year-old driver from Stettler, Alberta, tried to eat his own underwear in the hope that the cotton fabric would absorb the alcohol before he took a breathalyzer test. Maybe it worked, because his test level was below the legal limit and he was acquitted.

Whistle While You Work

In 1934, Paul Williams of Nashville, Tennessee, placed four golf balls in his mouth and managed to whistle at the same time!

Melt Down

Originating at a campsite in Dorset, England, in 1997, cheese racing, as it's known, involves slices of processed cheese—still in their plastic wrapping—being thrown on to a hot barbeque by contestants. The cheese wrapper doesn't melt, and the first cheese slice to inflate, wins the cheese race!

Slippery Starter

Tequila-flavored lollipops contain caterpillars or scorpions.

BORED WITH BEANS on toast? Then, for a while, Edible, a restaurant in London, England, was the place to eat!

Created by Todd Dalton, from Louisiana, Edible offered cuisine for those with an open mind. As well as boiled rattlesnake, customers could try such delicacies as alligator stew and chocolate-covered scorpions. Sadly, Londoners' stomachs weren't up to the challenge, and Edible is now closed.

If you spy a fly in your soup, just count yourself lucky that you didn't order piranha fish and chips, or beer-battered locusts!

Chef Dan Craven boils a rattlesnake to make a rattlesnake chili.

27

Eating his Words

As a stunt to launch the 2005 edition of This Diary Will Change Your Life, *22-year-old Londoner Will Parkinson took the wacky diary's advice to "eat this book" literally!*

Champion Chomper

Sonya Thomas, aged 36, of Alexandria, Virginia, only joined the International Federation of Competitive Eating in 2003, but the 105-lb (48-kg) rookie has already set records. These include eating 8.4 lbs (3.8 kg) of baked beans in under three minutes, 167 chicken wings in 32 minutes, 11 lbs (5 kg) of cheesecake in 9 minutes, 65 eggs in under 7 minutes, 38 lobsters in 12 minutes, and 432 oysters in 10 minutes.

Fruity Heirloom

Some families pass down jewelry from generation to generation, but Margie Clark of Oklahoma, is giving her kids a shrivelled orange. The shrunken, rock-hard, nearly petrified piece of fruit has been in her family since 1921 when it was given to her father by his sister, then stored in a trunk.

Hot Favorite

Chicago-based Vienna Beef unveiled a 37-ft 2-in (11-m) long hot dog at the 2004 Taste of Chicago festival. The monster wiener was garnished with 1 gal (4 l) of mustard, 1 gal (4 l) of green relish, 140 tomato slices, 4 lbs (2 kg) of chopped onions, and 70 pickle spears.

Cutting the Carbs

Jack LaLanne, 90, regarded by many as "the godfather of fitness," still works out for two hours a day, seven days a week. Ever since the age of 15, LaLanne has eaten a diet high in fruits and vegetables. Apparently, he hasn't had a sugary dessert since 1929.

Helped by other ingredients, such as bread, jam, banana and vanilla milkshakes, beetroot, tomato ketchup, and Coke, Will successfully consumed the entire book in seven hours!

A Cracking Idea

Competitors in the 4th of July sidewalk egg fry at Oatman, Arizona, cook eggs on the sidewalk using just the heat of the midday sun.

WHAT'S THE BEEF?

- When the first McDonald's opened in Russia, in 1990, more than 20,000 Muscovites queued to sample the wares

- The first hamburgers in the U.S.A. were served in New Haven, Connecticut, at Louis' Lunch sandwich shop in 1895. Owner Louis Lassen didn't like to waste excess beef, so he ground it, grilled it, and served it between two slices of bread

- There are an average of 178 sesame seeds on a McDonald's Big Mac bun

- In 1982, the town of Rutland, North Dakota, made a 3,591 lb (1,629 kg) hamburger, which was eaten by approximately 8,000 people

- In 1968, the Big Macs cost 49 cents (25 pence)

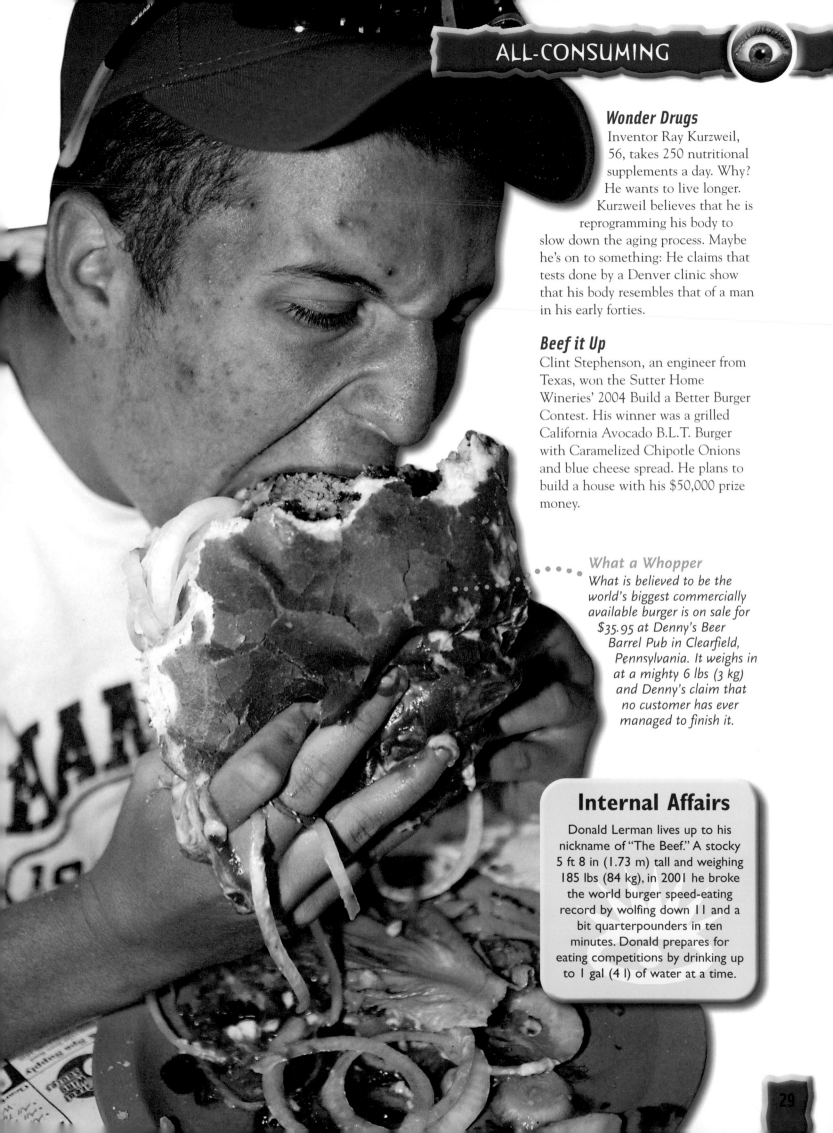

Wonder Drugs

Inventor Ray Kurzweil, 56, takes 250 nutritional supplements a day. Why? He wants to live longer. Kurzweil believes that he is reprogramming his body to slow down the aging process. Maybe he's on to something: He claims that tests done by a Denver clinic show that his body resembles that of a man in his early forties.

Beef it Up

Clint Stephenson, an engineer from Texas, won the Sutter Home Wineries' 2004 Build a Better Burger Contest. His winner was a grilled California Avocado B.L.T. Burger with Caramelized Chipotle Onions and blue cheese spread. He plans to build a house with his $50,000 prize money.

What a Whopper

What is believed to be the world's biggest commercially available burger is on sale for $35.95 at Denny's Beer Barrel Pub in Clearfield, Pennsylvania. It weighs in at a mighty 6 lbs (3 kg) and Denny's claim that no customer has ever managed to finish it.

Internal Affairs

Donald Lerman lives up to his nickname of "The Beef." A stocky 5 ft 8 in (1.73 m) tall and weighing 185 lbs (84 kg), in 2001 he broke the world burger speed-eating record by wolfing down 11 and a bit quarterpounders in ten minutes. Donald prepares for eating competitions by drinking up to 1 gal (4 l) of water at a time.

PUMPKiN PaddLers

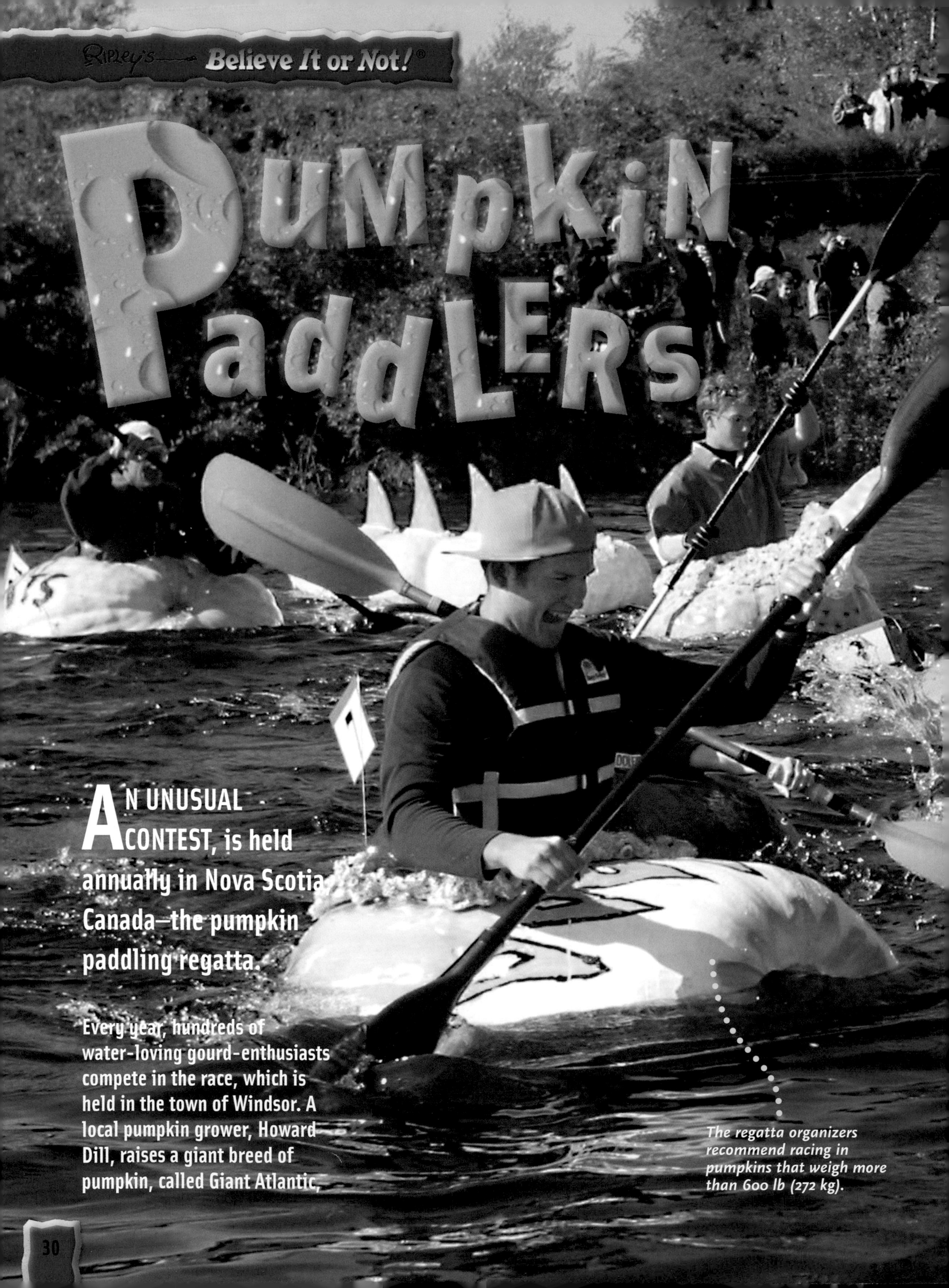

AN UNUSUAL
CONTEST, is held
annually in Nova Scotia,
Canada—the pumpkin
paddling regatta.

Every year, hundreds of
water-loving gourd-enthusiasts
compete in the race, which is
held in the town of Windsor. A
local pumpkin grower, Howard
Dill, raises a giant breed of
pumpkin, called Giant Atlantic,

*The regatta organizers
recommend racing in
pumpkins that weigh more
than 600 lb (272 kg).*

and rather than wasting the hollowed-out flesh after selling the seeds, gives them to contestants of the regatta so that they can further shape them to their own requirements. Not only do contestants have to bring their own wetsuits in order to compete, they must also carve out the insides to create a cockpit.

Experienced pumpkin paddler Chip Peterson dons a helmet made out of a pumpkin.

Pull Some Strings

Made using 18 gal (45 l) of olive oil, 1,100 lbs (500 kg) of flour, and 1,800 eggs, this fettuccine took the record in 1997 as the world's longest noodle in Singapore. Forty chefs spent five days in the kitchen cooking up the record-breaking pasta.

The hard work of the chefs and their assistants resulted in a staggering 3,776 ft (1,151 m) of the super strings!

Snail's Pace

A French seaweed collector retained one of the world's lesser-known sporting titles in August 2004—that of champion snail-spitter. Alain Jourden, aged 43, beat off 110 rivals from 14 different countries by propelling the live mollusk 30.8 ft (9.4 m) from a running start. Despite winning, however, he failed to match his own existing world record of 34.1 ft (10.4 m) because of some adverse wind conditions on the Brittany coast.

Pride of Lions

During their annual pancake festival in 2002, members of the Lubbock Lions Club in Lubbock, Texas, made 30,724 pancakes in just eight hours.

Red Alert

Nicholas Huenefeld of Ohio can swallow 24 oz (680 g) of ketchup in one sitting.

Carton Character

Anthony Key from Bath, England, created a sculpture called Female Buddha *using only chinese takeaway cartons!*

Sausage Feat

A village in Northern Serbia displayed a 3,280-ft (1,011-m) long sausage during a traditional meat festival in 1997.

U.S.A.
Arizona

In Tombstone, it's illegal for men and women over the age of 18 to have less than one missing tooth visible when smiling.

Baker's Oven
Ivan "Chamouni" Chalbert baked more than bread in his 400° F (200°C) oven! The 19th century Russian baker could withstand the same heat that thoroughly cooked raw meat.

BAKER IRON WORKS
LOS ANGELES

Ripley's®
"CHAMOUNI" THE BAKER
EXHIBIT NO: 1106
COULD CLIMB INSIDE HIS OWN OVEN AT
EXTREMELY HIGH TEMPERATURES

InDex

ACKNOWLEDGMENTS

Jacket (t/l) Tony Larkin/Rex Features; (b/l) Mimmo Frassineti/Rex Features; (b/r) Rex Features

4 Tony Larkin/Rex Features; 6 (t/r, b/c) Tony Larkin/Rex Features; 7 (t/r) A Rodriguez/Rex Features, (b/r) EDPpics/Hocknell/Rex Features; 8 (b) Henry Romero/Reuters; 9 (t) Adrian Sherratt/Rex Features; 11 (t/r) Mimmo Frassineti/Rex Features, (b/l) Paul Cooper/Rex Features; 12 (t/r) Assignments Photographers/Rex Features, (b/c) Toshifiumi Kitamura/AFP/Getty Images; 13 (b) 24/7 Media/Rex Features; 14 (b) Mike Walker/Rex Features; 15 (t/r, b) Nigel Tisdall/Rex Features; 16 (t/l) NWI/Rex Features; 17 SWS/Rex Features; 18 (b) Ian Patrick/Rex Features; 19 (t/r) Brendan Beirne/Rex Features; 22 (b) Assignments Photographers/Rex Features; 23 (b) John Chapple/Rex Features; 24 (t/r) HO/Reuters, (b) Sipa Press/Rex Features; 25 (b) Eriko Sugita/Reuters; 27 (t/r, b/r) Nils Jorgensen/Rex Features, (c) Gerry Penny/AFP/Getty Images Photo; 28 Ray Tang/Rex Features; 29 Rex Features; 30 (dp, b) Norm Betts/Rex Features; 32 (t/r, c) Reuters, (b) Rowan Griffiths/Rex Features.

All other photos are from Ripley's Entertainment Inc.
Every attempt has been made to acknowledge correctly and contact copyright holders and we apologize
in advance for any unintentional errors or omissions, which will be corrected in future editions.